Printed in the United States of America.

ISBN: 979-8-9950633-1-5

Whispers of the Runes

A Journey of Inner Wisdom

By

Tibor T. Farkas

Dedication

To my wife, Olesea, whose love, patience, and constant encouragement have guided and uplifted me at every step of this journey. Your presence is my greatest source of strength and inspiration.

To Aina, who first opened the sacred path of the runes before me, and to all my friends who took part in my rune readings, sharing their energy, curiosity, and insight along the way.

And to the All-Father, the eternal teacher, whose whispers became my inspiration and whose wisdom flows through every word within these pages.

"Let no man carve runes to cast a spell,
Save first he learn to read them well."

-Viking poet -

Table of Contents

Foreword

I have always been drawn to the search for spiritual wisdom, though that wasn't always the case. I can look back and see how the journey has evolved over time, but in my earlier years, I was a skeptic - one of the worst, in fact. At the time, I didn't believe in spirituality, faith, or religion. I would even make sarcastic jokes about those who did. However, life has a way of teaching us lessons we don't expect. Over the years, through personal experiences, I began to see the beauty in spirituality, and what was once a subject of ridicule became a deep, uplifting pursuit of truth.

My journey has taken me through various traditions: the ancient teachings of Kabbalah, yoga, and Buddhism. I read many books that opened my mind, including *The Alchemist* by Paulo Coelho and the works of Carlos Castaneda, which became favorites of mine. These practices and writings left a lasting impression on me, guiding me deeper into the exploration of consciousness and spiritual insight.

But the turning point in my journey came through an unexpected source - the runes. A dear friend of mine from New York, who was an avid student of the runes, introduced them to me. Though I had heard of the runes before, I had never engaged with them on a deep level. During a session she guided for my wife and me, she encouraged us to meditate on the runes, to see what insights we might gather.

It was during that very first meditation that my life changed. As I connected with the runes, I was introduced to the All-Father, Odin himself. It was a meeting unlike anything I had ever experienced. His presence was so profound, so powerful, that I found myself moved to tears. It was as though I had entered into a relationship with something ancient and wise beyond comprehension. I felt Odin guiding me, teaching me about the runes, and sharing knowledge that seemed far beyond my own understanding.

At that moment, I knew there was something deeper happening. This was not just a meditation, it was a call to document the insights I was receiving. From that day onward, I felt an obligation - no, a privilege - to write down everything I was learning. Odin had opened a door, and I was simply the messenger, tasked with sharing his wisdom with the world.

This book is the result of that journey.

Introduction

The runes originate from the depths beneath the World Tree's roots, Yggdrasil. To communicate with them and benefit from the wisdom they provide, we need to reach down to the bottom of the shadows of ourselves. It requires dedication and commitment to the search for true knowledge and the unshaken determination to be honest, and authentic to ourselves.

Once we can make this sacrifice, we can reap the rewards of the deep knowledge acquired from the runes.

Working with the runes can be a wonderful experience filled with eye-opening revelations and insights into every aspect of life.

In this book, I invite you on a magical journey to the realm of self-exploration with the guidance of the runes through which you can find the long-awaited answers to many questions buried deep within *your heart*.

I.

Origins of the Runes

Odin's Sacrifice: The Birth of the Runes

In the mists of the primordial world, long before men knew the language of the gods, there stood one among them who revered not power or wealth, but something far greater - knowledge. Odin, the All-Father, with one eye cast into the abyss of existence and the other fixed upon the mysteries of the cosmos, knew that knowledge was the key to all things. It was not power that he sought, but the truth, hidden in the vastness of the unknown. For Odin, to know was to live, and to seek was to ascend.

Hanging from the great World Tree, Yggdrasil, Odin sacrificed himself not for glory, but for wisdom - the deepest secret of all creation. With his spear piercing his side, he endured nine nights of silence, suspended between life and death. And it was in that moment, when flesh became weak, that the runes revealed themselves. Symbols of pure knowledge, they fell like fragments of the stars into his hands, granting him the power to decipher the fabric of existence.

The runes, broken free by Odin's sacrifice, were more than just symbols - they were tools, gifts of the divine. These symbols held the secrets of the universe, offering insight into the past, present, and future. And through them, mankind could grasp at the eternal mystery that lay just beyond their mortal reach. For while men are perishable, knowledge is eternal, and through the runes, the mortal hand may reach toward the infinite.

Odin knew that in gifting the runes to men, he was offering them the greatest adventure of all - the pursuit of knowledge. For it is through this quest that we, fragile beings of flesh and bone, can sit at the feet of the gods. The runes are more than mere marks on stone - they are the keys to becoming something greater. Not gods, no, but seekers of the eternal, walking a path where the mystery of knowing is the most profound journey one can take.

There is no higher calling than to seek, and no greater reward than to know. This was Odin's gift to us - a reminder that we, too, can break through the barriers of our own understanding. We may never fully grasp all the answers, but with the runes, we are given the tools to explore the mysteries of our existence, guided by the wisdom of the **All-Father** himself.

History of The Elder Futhark

The tale of Odin's sacrifice for the runes is rich with mystery, yet it is only the beginning of their journey into the world of men. While the runes came to us through the divine hands of the All-Father, their place in history is deeply intertwined with the people of Northern Europe. Carved into stone, bone, and wood, these symbols were not only sacred but practical - a means of communication, protection, and power.

Historically, the runes first appeared during the early centuries of the Common Era, used by the Germanic tribes that roamed the forests and plains of Scandinavia, Germany, and Britain. These symbols, known as the Elder Futhark, were more than a mere alphabet. Each rune held layers of meaning, representing sounds, objects, and concepts that connected the material world to the spiritual.

The ancient peoples who wielded the runes saw them not only as a method of writing but as powerful talismans. Inscriptions were often used in rituals to invoke protection, seek guidance from the gods, or ensure success in battle. Warriors carved them into their weapons, believing that the very essence of the rune would give strength to their arm and courage to their heart. Farmers etched them into the earth to call upon the gods for bountiful harvests. These runes were alive, imbued with the essence of those who inscribed them, bridging the human and the divine.

Through centuries of use, the runes became both a link to the spiritual realms and a practical tool for survival. Their presence can still be felt in the remnants of runestones scattered across Northern Europe, standing as silent witnesses to the intertwining of myth and reality.

There is an abundant amount of information on the internet and in books about the interpretation and the meaning of each runic symbol. The purpose of this book is to invite the reader to the esoteric, spiritual realm of the runes and highlight the insights that can be extracted from the essence of their deep meaning.

The All-Father

Odin is not just a figure of ancient myth, far removed from our modern world. In my own journey of seeking knowledge and connection to the divine, I found myself drawn to him, to understand the All-Father beyond the stories. In a deep meditation, the veil between worlds seemed to thin, and there, in the space between the conscious and the unknown, I saw him.

Odin revealed himself to me not just as a god of light, but as a being who holds both the darkness and the light in perfect balance. To look into his eyes was to feel the weight of his endless wisdom, with a sharp, cunning edge that shone just beneath the surface. There was always a dangerous glint, a knowing look that made it clear he could outwit anyone if he wished. But in that moment, I knew he would not use that power against me - for I was there to learn, and Odin is, above all, a guide for those who seek knowledge.

He is not a god for the faint-hearted, yet it is not only strength that Odin reveres. While deep knowledge and truth may demand bravery and sacrifice, there are many paths to wisdom. Courage can take many forms - it can be the strength to face difficult truths, but it can also be the cleverness to navigate through challenges when strength alone isn't enough. Odin embodies both. Sometimes, it is not power that is needed, but wit, and Odin knows this well. His cunning is as much a part of him as his bravery, reminding us that there is always more than one way to reach our goals.

In my meditations, Odin often appeared with his two ravens, Huginn and Muninn, perched nearby. They are his eyes and ears, flying across the realms to bring him the thoughts and memories of the world. At his side, his two wolves, Geri and Freki, stood ever watchful, symbols of his strength and loyalty. And in his right hand, Odin always held his long spear, Gungnir, a weapon that represented both his authority and his readiness for battle.

Standing before him, I felt so small, often no higher than his ankles, and in these visions, I would find myself flying just to meet his gaze. His presence was so powerful, his energy so vibrant, that to be near him felt like standing in the heart of a storm. Yet, even in his imposing presence, there was kindness - a sense that, for those who seek truth with an open heart, Odin will always guide.

What struck me most was not his power, but his essence. Odin reveres knowledge above all else, and in his presence, I felt the pull of that same longing. It wasn't power or dominion he craved, but the truth that lies hidden behind the veil of existence. His was the pursuit of understanding, the ultimate adventure that never ends. And as I sat there, in the stillness of my meditation, I realized that this was the gift he offers us: the runes, not just as symbols, but as keys to the mysteries of the universe.

In that moment, I understood that the pursuit of knowledge is not just a task for the divine, but for all of us. Through seeking, we rise. Through understanding, we transcend the limits of our fragile human existence. And it was in that space, with Odin before me, that I felt we, too, can step closer to the divine by embracing the mysteries he revealed to us.

Odin is a god of polarities. He is the manliest of men, strong and commanding, yet he also walks the line between the light and the shadow. He does not merely celebrate those with courage in battle or in life; he also respects those who use their wit, their intelligence, to overcome obstacles. It is this balance that makes him so powerful - he is both the fierce warrior and the clever strategist, the protector of wisdom and the **keeper of secrets**.

Introduction of the Runes

As divine beings, we enter this world with a desire to express the vastness of our essence. Yet, the very language we use to communicate is inherently limited. Words, though powerful, can only touch the surface of what we truly feel and know deep within. No matter how carefully we choose them, they often fall short of expressing the full depth of our inner truth. They confine our emotions, our thoughts, and our divine creativity into rigid structures that cannot fully capture the boundless nature of who we are.

This is where the magic of the runes begins to transcend ordinary language. Each rune is not merely an alphabetical symbol - it is a living, breathing embodiment of entire aspects of life. In a single rune lies the essence of creation, challenge, or transformation. These symbols carry within them the whispers of ancient knowledge and the intricate patterns woven into the very fabric of existence. When we work with the runes, we tap into a language that surpasses mere words, connecting us directly to the core truths of life itself.

To understand the runes is to open a gateway to deeper self-expression, one that can touch your heart and soul if you approach it with a willingness to see beyond the limitations of speech. The runes have the power to communicate with the very essence of life. If you are hungry for knowledge and have the courage to delve into their mysteries, they can illuminate the path before you in ways that transcend ordinary understanding. This is the magic and the reward of working with the runes.

The Runes and the Multiverse

The ancient Norse people, often regarded as warriors and seafarers, had a much deeper connection to the cosmos than we might initially believe. Their spiritual beliefs, rooted in a profound connection with nature and the divine, revolved around the understanding that reality extended beyond the physical world. The Norse cosmology was built upon the idea of multiple realms - nine worlds, to be precise - that coexisted simultaneously, each influencing and interacting with the others. These worlds were bound together by the great cosmic tree, Yggdrasil, a representation of interconnectedness that transcended time, space, and existence.

While we, in modern times, might call this concept a "multiverse" through the lens of quantum physics, the Vikings and other Nordic peoples saw it as a spiritual truth. These realms were not theoretical; they were real places, existing alongside our own, and it was believed that the divine, the ancestors, and other spiritual beings resided within them. The Vikings had a keen awareness that reality was not singular, nor was it linear. Instead, they believed in an unfolding web of possibilities, each interconnected and accessible depending on one's awareness, actions, and intentions.

It is within this framework that the runes emerge as more than just an alphabet or a means of communication. They were powerful tools that acted as gateways to this multiverse, allowing individuals to access the wisdom and energy flowing through the various realms. Runes were a form of language not only for the gods but for the very fabric of reality itself. By casting or invoking runes, one could open themselves to the currents of the multiverse, gaining insight into the ever-shifting threads of fate, or "Wyrd."

The future, as the Vikings understood it, was never set in stone. Much like the modern concept of multiple realities or timelines, the Norse believed in the idea of potential outcomes rather than fixed destiny. The Norns, who were said to weave the threads of fate, influenced the course of events, but they did not impose a singular path. Individuals had the power to shape their destiny through their thoughts, actions, and intentions, aligning themselves with different outcomes based on their current vibrational state.

When we use the runes today for divination, we are not asking them to tell us a definitive future. Instead, the runes act as mirrors, reflecting the energies and vibrations that currently dominate our internal and external worlds. Each rune, when drawn or cast, reveals the potential pathways that exist within the multiverse at this very moment. It tells us not what will happen but what could happen if we continue on our current trajectory.

Much like how modern science explores the idea of quantum states, where the observer's actions influence the outcome, the Vikings understood that our thoughts, feelings, and energies create vibrations that ripple through the multiverse. The runes tap into this vibrational level and guide us toward understanding what we are likely to manifest based on where we are right now, energetically and mentally. In other words, they help us understand the current trajectory of our reality - both present and future - without locking us into a fixed fate.

In this way, the runes are tools for navigating the multiverse. When you consult the runes for guidance, you are tapping into the energies that currently shape your life. The runes reveal the dominant influences at play - whether from the past, present, or potential futures - and allow you to consciously engage with these energies. This is a critical understanding: the runes are not there to dictate your future, but to give you insight into your current vibrational state and help you make choices that align with your desired outcome.

Therefore, casting the runes is an act of co-creation with the universe. The moment the runes are drawn, they are reflecting the vibrational level you are currently embodying, showing you the potential paths you are already walking. But, just as the Vikings understood, you have the power to change course. The runes, in essence, are bridges between the conscious and subconscious mind. They allow us to communicate with the parts of ourselves that we may not fully comprehend or access directly, offering a glimpse into the deeper layers of our being and the energies we are emitting into the multiverse.

In the hands of those who seek wisdom, the runes become an essential guide for navigating the vast, interconnected realities of the multiverse. They are not rigid markers of destiny, but rather dynamic indicators of the infinite possibilities that lie ahead. The power of the runes lies not in their ability to predict the future, but in their ability to illuminate the present, to reveal the energies at play, and to provide insight into how we might shape our path forward in alignment with the universe.

II.

The runic system of the Elder Futhark

The Elder Futhark consists of 24 runic symbols. For rune casting and divination, there is a 25th "symbol" of an empty stone, piece of wood, or card, representing "Odin's Rune," the mystery rune. These 24 runic symbols are further divided into three sections with eight sets of runes each. These are called the Aetts.

The first ætt is Freya's ætt, which represents fertility, growth, prosperity, and the foundational elements of life. Freya, the goddess of love and fertility, is associated with this group, and the runes often relate to the beginnings of things, like creation and fertility.

The second ætt is Heimdall's ætt (also sometimes called Hagal's ætt in other traditions), and it represents challenges, protection, and the trials we face in life. Heimdall, the watchman of the gods, symbolizes vigilance and guardianship. This ætt often deals with overcoming obstacles and understanding the balance between destruction and renewal.

The third ætt is Tyr's ætt. This one symbolizes justice, duty, war, and sacrifice. Tyr is the god of law and heroic glory, and his ætt deals with themes of responsibility, spiritual growth, and the strength needed for victory or honorable sacrifice.

These three ætts form a journey from the birth and growth of Freya's ætt, through the trials and struggles of Heimdall's ætt, to the ultimate challenges and duties represented by Tyr's ætt.

In this journey of life, we first enter the physical world as vessels of pure potential, brimming with the desire to express our true essence. The first ætt, Freya's ætt, symbolizes this sacred act of manifestation. Here, creativity flows like a river, carving paths of possibility. These eight runes represent the seeds we plant in the fertile soil of reality, nurturing them with our thoughts, desires, and actions until they bloom into tangible expressions of our inner light. It is a time of birth, growth, and the unfolding of our creative essence in this earthly realm.

As we walk the path of life, however, the winds of change begin to stir. The second ætt, Heimdall's ætt, ushers in the inevitable challenges, trials, and calamities that test the strength of our creations. Just as day cannot exist without night, so too must our expression be tempered by adversity. These eight runes are symbols of the storms we must weather, the obstacles we must overcome. Yet it is through these very struggles that we are refined, sharpened, and made whole, for every challenge holds the key to deeper understanding and resilience.

Finally, the third ætt, Tyr's ætt, leads us to the culmination of this sacred journey. Here, after facing the trials and tribulations of life, we are called to draw conclusions that align us with the higher truths of justice, balance, and wisdom. Tyr, the god of sacrifice and honor, teaches us that the final victory lies not in avoidance of hardship but in embracing the lessons it imparts. These eight runes are the compass that guides us toward integrity, urging us to act with truthfulness, courage, and balance in all we do. It is here that we find the true harmony between creation and challenge, between the individual and the collective.

The First Aett - Freya's Aettir

In Norse paganism, **Freyja** (in Old Norse meaning "(the) Lady") is a goddess associated with love, beauty, and fertility.

The First Aett represents the "Life Cycle"

The first set of runes represent the innermost qualities that are the basis of the creation, progression and the conclusion of our expression in the physical world.

Fehu

Wealth, luck, attraction

"Every question has within it the seeds of its own answer."

Fehu is the rune of wealth. True wealth is having everything we need or desire - surrounding ourselves with the essence of our true being manifested into material expressions such as objects, people, and circumstances that carry the vibration of well-being.

We came into this world to practice self-expression and self-gratification. Wealth is the way we measure our development in the manifested world. It is never something external; it always begins within. Wealth is an indicator of our inner progress. The deeper we connect with the infinite essence of our true self and draw power from within, the wealthier we become. The foundation of all wealth is energy, and this energy is love. The more we love, the wealthier we are.

Fehu, being the first symbol of the Elder Futhark, also represents new beginnings - an open mind ready to receive. It is the beginner's mindset: open, curious, free from judgment and expectation. It is the feeling of looking forward to something new with excitement and trust. When we are open and receptive, we receive abundance and become whole.

Fehu is the subtle, refined flow of divine energy - the substance of all that exists. It reminds us that every expression of life begins within us, waiting to be shared with the world.

Fehu is the key that unlocks the door of CREATION.

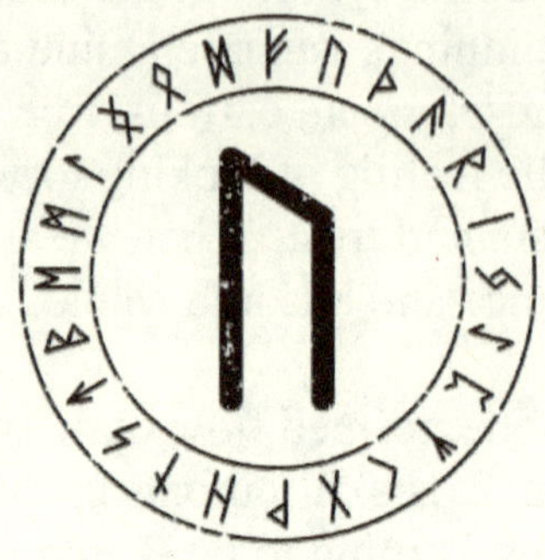

Uruz

Strength, endurance, vitality, manifestation

"Mind over matter, matter over mind."

Uruz is the rune of strength - strength of mind, strength of will, and strength of vitality. It is the embodiment of raw creative power and the determination that shapes physical matter and influences the material world. Strength is willpower in motion, the focused force that transforms invisible energy into tangible form.

Everything is energy, and this energy is shaped and directed by our will. Uruz helps us to awaken and harness this immense power, guiding us to mold our destiny with intention. Its essence is the wild, untamed energy of the Universe itself - an infinite source that can be invoked to bring health, success, abundance, and transformation into our lives.

Like a sword forged in fire, the energy of Uruz must be used with awareness. It holds tremendous power, yet requires mastery and restraint. Just as we would not use a sword for eating, but for defense or courage in battle, Uruz must be summoned when true strength is needed. The sword has two sharp edges - and so does Uruz - teaching us to wield power with balance, precision, and purpose.

When we set clear intentions and steer them with faith, Uruz becomes the ship that carries us toward our goals. We are the captains of this vessel, guided by will and determination. Through Uruz, we learn that nothing is beyond reach - because within us lies the strength from which anything is POSSIBLE.

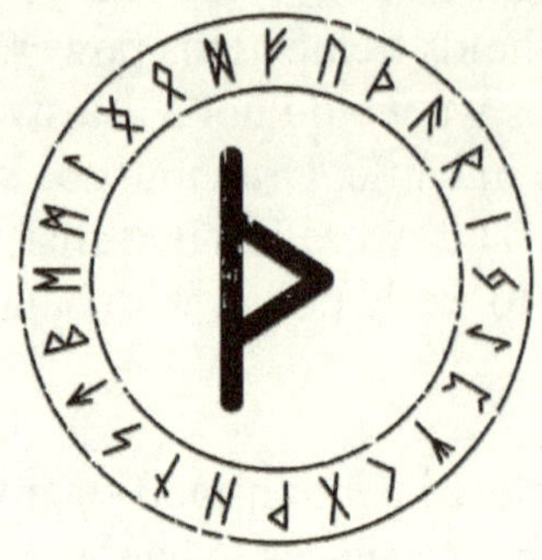

Thurisaz

Giant, lightning, protection, breaking down barriers

"To know the Divine, one must be still...
and wait, so when one is silent... and ready,
one may pass through this Gate."

Thurisaz is the rune of immense, unpredictable power - the kind that strikes suddenly, like lightning between earth and sky. It represents energy that cannot be controlled but can be harnessed in the right moment. When this force appears, we must be alert and ready to act, for it comes without warning and vanishes just as quickly.

When the conditions of life align, Thurisaz opens a flash of opportunity that can shatter stagnation and illuminate the path forward. If we find ourselves in turmoil or trapped by discomfort, the key is patience and awareness. By keeping a level mind, we can recognize the instant when the spark arrives - catch it, ride it, and break through the barriers that have confined us.

With time and mastery, we learn to call upon Thurisaz consciously. Its energy then comes like Thor's hammer, Mjolnir - sudden, powerful, and precise - moving us exactly where we need to be.

Thurisaz reminds us that opportunity is both a gift and a challenge. It tests our readiness to act in harmony with divine timing. This rune appears in the blink of an eye, offering transformation to those who are prepared. When we are grounded, present, and open, we can channel this lightning force to awaken our true potential and create lasting change.

Thurisaz is the opportunity that strikes in a single moment, revealing itself only ***when we are READY!***

Ansuz

Speech, wisdom, knowledge, divine inspiration

"Find your ears before you search for words."

Ansuz is the rune that connects us to the very fabric of reality, woven by the thoughts we form and expressed through the words we speak.
"In the beginning was the Word, and the Word was with God, and the Word was God."

The voice of wisdom we seek is the same divine voice that created this world. The answer is always around us - we simply need to stop, be still, and listen.

Speech is a sacred tool, a bridge between thought and manifestation. It is not the words themselves that hold power, but the intention and awareness behind them. Speaking transforms inner truth into outer creation. We always speak what we believe, therefore our speech is the reflection of our inner world.

Through speech, we connect. Through speech, we are known. Through speech, we inspire.
Truth and wisdom are sacred gifts of the divine. When spoken from the heart, they bless both the speaker and the listener. Each genuine word becomes an act of creation, carrying the resonance of divine purpose.

The rightly spoken word is a gift from our higher self to the world - a spark that shapes reality with love and clarity.

Our words ***create the WORLD!***

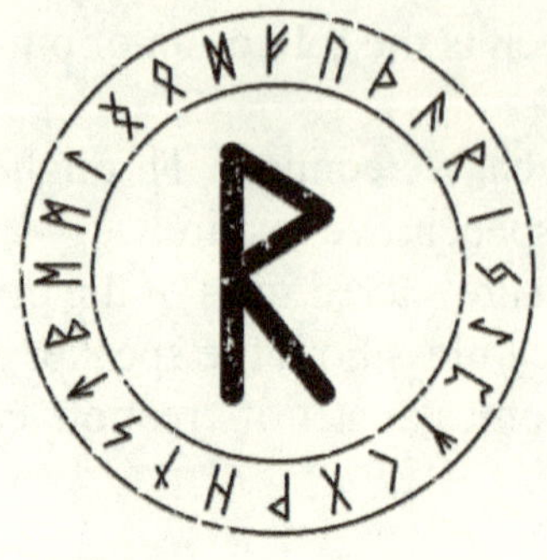

Raidho

Righteousness, inner balance, the journey of life, motion

"The journey is the destination."

Raidho is the rune of life itself - being in the everlasting moment, one heartbeat after another. It is about being in control of life, being in control of our thoughts and actions. When we drive a car, we don't just let it go wherever it wants; we drive it.

Focusing on Raidho will help us to drive the vehicle of our life. Life is movement - constant and endless motion that never stops. As our consciousness travels through the never-ending void filled with potentials waiting to be fulfilled, from the nothingness we dream and create the illusion of the world around us that manifests into shapes, forms, and circumstances that make us feel one way or another. But as our thoughts constantly change, so does the world around us. There is no beginning and there is no end. There is no destination, only constant manifestation.

This is the journey of our life, where the only control we have is what we think and how we act. Our actions cannot be wiser than our thoughts, and our thoughts cannot be wiser than our understanding.

Raidho is an incredibly positive rune that can help us be in charge of our destiny. We know what we want, and we know what we don't want. Simply paying attention to the road ahead and avoiding obstacles will take us far in the game of life. It is our proper decision-making, our moral compass, and the action steps we take that bring success and fulfillment.

Raidho is the rune of the right mindset followed by the right actions that take us to the RIGHT PLACE!

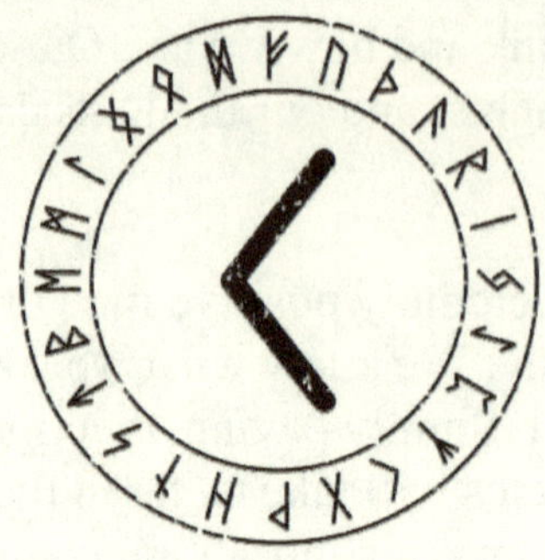

Kenaz

Torchlight, knowledge, clarity, experience

" To know what you know and what you do not know, that is true knowledge."

Kenaz is the rune of focused intention. It is born from the light of knowledge, which itself is the result of polarity. Polarity arises when the circumstances we experience and the circumstances we desire do not align. This tension creates friction - sparks that ignite the fire of awareness and the light of knowledge that guides us through the darkness of our cluttered minds.

Knowledge is honesty. It is the state of mind where we see things as they truly are, without denial or resistance. It is when the pure light of truth shines upon the darkness of ignorance created by our fears - fears that bind and limit us. When that light reveals everything, understanding follows.

Knowledge is power. Knowledge is truth. And truth is the path to freedom. Knowledge sets us free.

Kenaz reminds us that knowledge may come through experience in the physical world or through direct insight from within. This is why the rune takes the shape of a turned “V” - an opening, a channel between the inner world and the outer manifested world.

Our experiences are the conclusions drawn from observing our thoughts and actions as they take form in reality. When this outer knowledge merges with the inner spark of creativity, we gain the power to shape and form our destiny with the guided, steady torchlight of focused **INTENTION!**

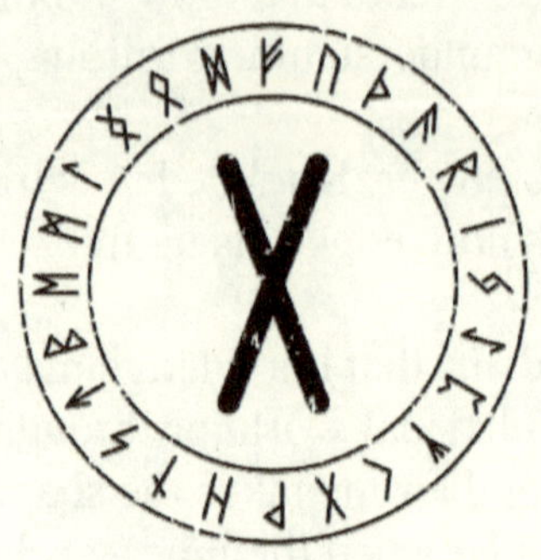

Gebo

Gift of giving and receiving, exchange, sacrifice

" Be a friend to your friend and repay each gift with a gift. Repay laughter with laughter, repay treachery with treachery."

Gebo represents the power of giving and receiving. When we are in the state of giving, we feel excited and alive, for in that moment we are connected to the divine source of **ALL THERE IS.** When we are in the state of receiving, we experience gratitude and appreciation. In true receiving, we feel a profound sense of self-worth - open to life and deserving of the blessings that come our way.

Through Gebo, we understand that we ourselves are the acting hand of the Universe - sometimes to give, sometimes to receive. When we give to others, we fulfill our divine role as channels of abundance. When we receive, we honor the same flow by allowing energy to return to us. Thus, the sacred circle of giving and receiving is complete.

Gebo also stands for balance and harmony. Everything in life is interconnected, and our actions inevitably ripple outward to affect others. It is therefore essential to strive for fairness, generosity, and gratitude in all relationships and exchanges.

Gebo reminds us that the true measure of self-worth lies not in what we receive, but in what we give. Every exchange is a reflection of who we are and the energy we bring into the world.

Gebo is the crossing of paths where our interactions with others will shape the image of who we REALLY ARE!

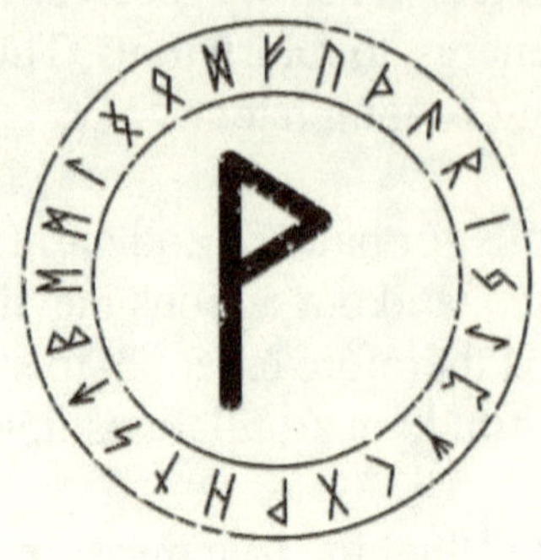

Wunjo

Happiness, joy, harmony, perfection, friendship

" A heart full of joy gives good advice."

Wunjo is the rune of wholeness. When we are whole - balanced in mind, elevated in spirit, and healthy in body - we resonate with the vibration of Source energy and naturally experience joy and happiness.

When we are happy, we are fully present in the moment, joyfully witnessing the unfolding of creation. Wunjo is the single most positive rune; it represents all the goodness that life has to offer - unity within communities, strong bonds of friendship, and harmony within families.

When we are connected with Source, our thoughts and emotions align with divine order, allowing abundance and peace to unfold naturally in our lives. This connection becomes the bridge through which joy flows freely, transforming our perception and bringing clarity to every aspect of our existence.

Wunjo reminds us that joy is not something we chase but something we allow by returning to our natural state of balance and gratitude. When we are whole, life responds with abundance and beauty.

Being in the state of joy and happiness we are connected to our higher selves and effortlessly carry out the creation of a wonderful and prosperous reality around us…

…so, we can **ENJOY!**

The Second Aett - Heimdallr's Aett

In Norse paganism, **Heimdallr** (in Old Norse meaning "world-brightener") is a god who is often seen as a symbol of vigilance, protection, and illumination.

The Second Aett represents the destructive and external forces.

The second set of runes represent the external forces and circumstances that are posed upon our expression in this world, through which we can seek enlightenment and understanding of all things.

Hagalaz

Acceptance, surrender, opportunity

" Don't try to fix what we should break before it breaks us."

Hagalaz is the rune of ultimate truth - the truth within our soul that remains untouched by the efforts of the mind.

Hagalaz breaks down the illusions that stand between us and the truth we must see within ourselves. Often, we become carried away by the constant stream of thoughts that - moving in a linear and relentless pattern - pull us forward into the realities we create.

These are the thoughts of the mind, the voice of the ego. And when those thoughts fall out of alignment with the true desires and will of the higher self, a correction becomes necessary.

This correction often comes as a hailstorm of events or emotional revelations - powerful experiences that shatter false patterns and bring us back to the truth of our soul. Though it may feel harsh or chaotic, this cleansing storm clears the path for renewal and realignment.

In every upheaval, there lies opportunity.

Hagalaz is the opportunity to rediscover our divine path and return to the truth of our SOUL!

Nauthiz

Necessity, friction, resistance, urgency

" Necessity is the mother of invention."

Nauthiz is the rune of cosmic resistance. From the most inner core of being we naturally resist negative feelings. This is why we feel "bad", uncomfortable in situations that are not in our favor. This resistance creates an equal need, a necessity to counter the negative feeling and replace it with a more positive one. Without the feel of "need", we wouldn't have the desire for the actions that we have to take in order to change our circumstances which make us feel uncomfortable.

Often times we find ourselves having negative thoughts of fear and worry about things in our life that we have no control over. With the help of our feel of "need" to thrive and survive, we become creative and innovative, so we come up with ideas and solutions to overcome the challenges that we face. Nautiz reminds us that friction is not our enemy but a teacher guiding us toward growth. Every challenge we face has the potential to awaken our hidden strength and inner ingenuity. When we align with Nauthiz, we learn to channel resistance into movement and necessity into creation. It is in the heat of struggle that transformation begins, and through that process, we emerge wiser, stronger, and more capable than before.

Nauthiz is the key we **NEED** to unlock the door of innovation!

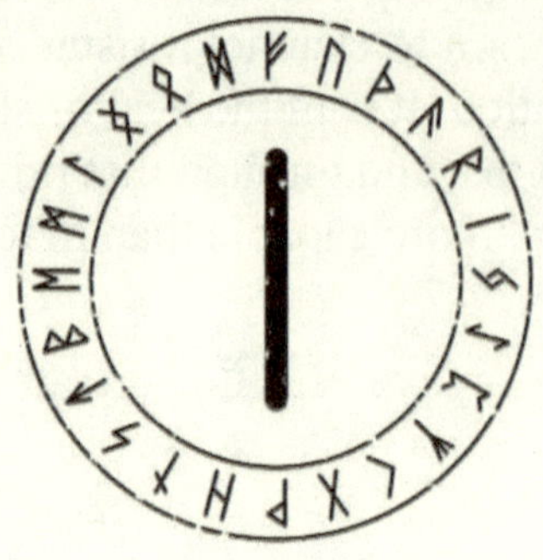

Isa

Stillness, self-control, identity, focus

" Ice only appears to stop a river's flow."

Isa is the rune of stillness. It is the moment when the whole world stops and our consciousness is focused into one single point, a point of interest, a subject of great importance. It is a fine line where our consciousness makes a transition from the state of undefined possibilities to the state of defined choice. This requires a great deal of concentration.

This state of mind can be experienced in extreme sports like rock climbing, wingsuit flying or high speed racing to name a few, where one little mistake, one slip of focus can cause detrimental effects.

This single point of focus is the conception of the ego. It is the undivided focus of the divine self into one single entity that causes the illusion of separation of self from the rest of creation. The birth of the ego and it's existence in the illusion of separation is absolutely necessary to gain those experiences that can be acquired only from this point of view.

Since the very existence of our identity is based on this concentrated focus of divine self, it is very easy to get lost in the illusion of the ego. This self-centeredness creates a whole new world from it's own perspective and our racing mind carries itself away into a million different directions and desires in a linear pattern, one moment after the other.

Isa can help us to brake this pattern by "fighting fire with fire", and by using a self-initiated focused concentration into one point, opening up the window to the view of the true world, a world where we are all one with the Universe.

Isa is the fine line, the **FROZEN MOMENT**, the gate breached by our focus where our consciousness transcends from the ego to the divine self!

Jera

Harvest, patience, time

"Patience up to a point. Know your time, but work your wyrd always."

Jera is the rune of patience and time. In this physical reality we are bound by the illusion of time. We perceive our life and the world around us in a linear pattern. One moment after the other. As we move along this pattern, we sow the seeds of our thoughts which fall into the fertile ground of our subconscious mind where they manifest into our reality over time. Our thoughts are like seeds that originate in our minds, and by expressing them through words and actions, they take shape in the world around us. This is a powerful process, yet it operates within its own natural boundaries, much like how the Earth orbits the Sun.

The illusion of time is absolutely necessary for our consciousness to be able to perceive, break down and process the concept of manifestation. Every thought and idea in one shape or form will present itself to us to reflect upon. What we sow is what we will harvest.

Through the virtue of patience, we can learn to master the flow of time. Jera, the rune of harvest and cycles, guides us to stay grounded and fully present, appreciating each beautiful moment in the creation of our world.

Jera reminds us that manifestation in this reality is a sacred procession, moving with the rhythm of cosmic order where all things emerge in their **DESTINED SEASON** and woven into the eternal fabric of life itself!

Eihwaz

Perseverance, endurance, life and death

" There is a time to be born, and a time to die, and the time in between is life itself."

Eihwaz, symbolized by the yew tree, is the rune that embodies the spirit of perseverance.

It represents the unyielding willpower that remains constant, even in the face of adversity. Eihwaz is the consciousness that transcends the illusions of life and encompasses the awareness of existence from the beginning of time until the end of time and beyond.

Throughout our lives, we all seek fulfillment in various aspects such as personal growth, financial stability, family, and love. Eihwaz reminds us that our journey towards fulfillment starts from the seeds of our desires at the roots of the world tree

Yggdrasil. As we navigate through life, we encounter numerous choices and seemingly endless possibilities that guide us along the trunk of the tree.

Eventually, we reach the crown of the tree, where the branches extend and bear the fruit of our efforts. It is here where we can look down and see life from a broader perspective and gain a deeper understanding.

Eihwaz teaches us that perseverance is essential to reach our destination, and it is our innate gift that helps us face the challenges and appreciate the blessings of life.

Eihwaz is the immortal fire of our will through which we can transcend our essence of being from the trials of life to **ENLIGHTMENT!**

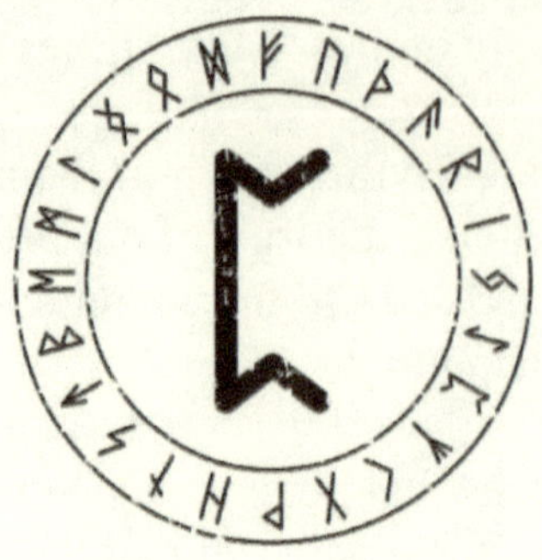

Perthro

Luck, chance, fate, mystery

" The unknown has never let me down."

Perthro is the rune of fate. There are two things that are certain in life. What was and what is. The future is the realm of endless possibilities. As we live our life from moment to moment, there is always a certain key emotion in any given time which determines our actions we take. This emotion is what we feel when we anticipate the future. It could be hope, excitement, ease and happiness, or anxiety, hopelessness and fear.

The particular way we feel is the seed we put into the soil of manifestation, and the more of the same seeds we sow, the more of the same fruits we will harvest in the upcoming days, weeks, months and years. Therefore, it is very important to be conscious about the way we feel in any given moment.

Perthro reminds us that the future is not set in stone, and in any moment anything is possible. If we realize that we are the creators of our reality, we are given a chance to create a much favorable future for ourselves.

Perthro is the chance that is given to us in every moment to fulfill our **DESTINY!**

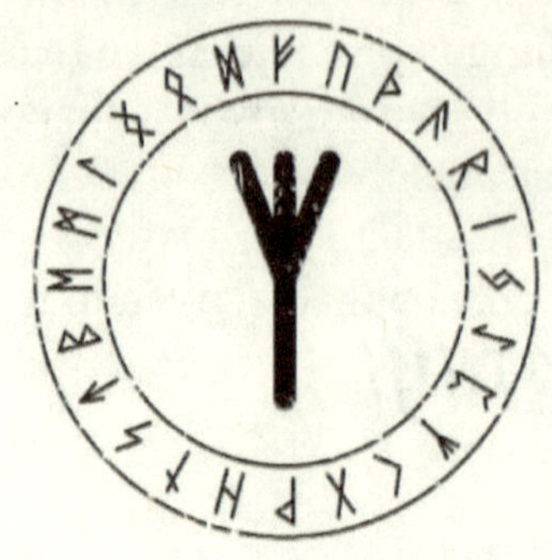

Algiz

Protection, higher self, divinity

" Fear has its place in every heart.
Courage is only a response."

Algiz is the rune of protection. It is the divine bridge that connects us with our higher self. We create our word in every moment. The seeds of creation originate from the very essence of our thoughts. These thoughts are to be felt, and our feelings are to be expressed. Often times we find ourselves feeling afraid of situations, events, people, etc. It is the result of our uncontrolled thought pattern that caused the creation of the reality we fear. Those events and circumstances show up to reflect our thoughts.

With the aid of Algiz, we can connect to the higher, divine part of ourselves and subconsciously take control of those thoughts, thus resulting the creation of much favorable events and circumstances reflecting the absence of fear.

We can call this “protection”.

Algiz is the divine link that connects us to our higher will and this connection results in the **PREVENTION** of misfortunes caused be the uncontrolled thought patterns created be our lower self.

Sowilo

Victory, guidance, mastery, wholeness

" The guide leads you to the doorway, then waits for your return."

Sowilo is the rune of transformation. It represents the Sun's energy and power. This power transforms possibilities into results by the act of our will. Just like the power of our Sun, which provides heat and light for all life on Earth. Every life form exist because they have the will to live.

Our Sun is a star. It's gravity and energy holds our whole solar system together. When we harness the power of a star through Sowilo, we become the masters of our life. We become whole. We keep winning, winning and winning. Mastery from the other hand requires discipline, consistency and the strength of our will.

Through the virtue of these attributes, our negative behaviors,- like procrastination, laziness, hesitation-, transform into a vital and dynamic force of creation. Under the light of Sowilo, these stagnant energies become fuel for creation. Procrastination transforms into purposeful action. Laziness gives way to vitality. Hesitation evolves into decisive momentum.

When we embrace Sowilo's energy, we tap into a limitless source of inspiration and power, a reminder that we are not merely passive observers in life but active participants in shaping it. By embodying the virtues of Sowilo, we align ourselves with the Sun's example: steady, life-giving, and unstoppable. In doing so, we unlock our highest potential and step into the **RADIANT FORCE** of our true selves.

The Third Aett - Tyr's Aett

In Norse paganism, **Heimdallr** (in Old Norse meaning "world-brightener") is a god who is often seen as a symbol of vigilance, protection, and illumination.

The Third Aett represents the internal and divine forces.

The third set of runes represent the higher spiritual awareness within us - the awakening of divine consciousness, self-mastery, and the realization of one's true purpose through wisdom and inner transformation.

Tiwaz

Justice, sacrifice, principles, spiritual warrior

"What is higher than the self is the Self become Higher."

Tiwaz is the rune of justice, honor and balance. It is the highest quality of self-expression in the physical world. It serves as a beacon of light amidst the opposing forces in the unfolding of creation. It is a beacon of a very distant, deep and serene force. It is represented in our physical world by the North Star which helps us to navigate our way on our journey of life and the ever-unfolding expansion of our soul. The separation of polarities- good vs bad, light vs darkness - yields to the creation of a dualistic multiverse which is the fertile ground for the seeds of endless possibilities and versatile experiences for the soul. Tiwaz is here to remind us that with self-discipline and the mastery of ourselves we can keep our gaze on the stars and follow our dreams while we can walk with solid feet on the ground and live and honorable lifestyle. Courage is the very essence of honesty. Without courage we are unable to see deeply within ourselves and recognize our weaknesses that keep us from a fulfilled and happy life. Tiwaz will help us to find our courage in the darkest hours of our soul where the towering waves of fear of the unknown and the doubts of ourselves crash against the ship of our unfolding life. It will shine as a bright star in the night sky, filling our heart with hope, our mind with clarity and our will with determination.

Tiwaz is the beacon of light for the spiritual warrior within us who is truthful, honest and just, therefore our path we walk is a righteous one that always leads us to **SUCCESS!**

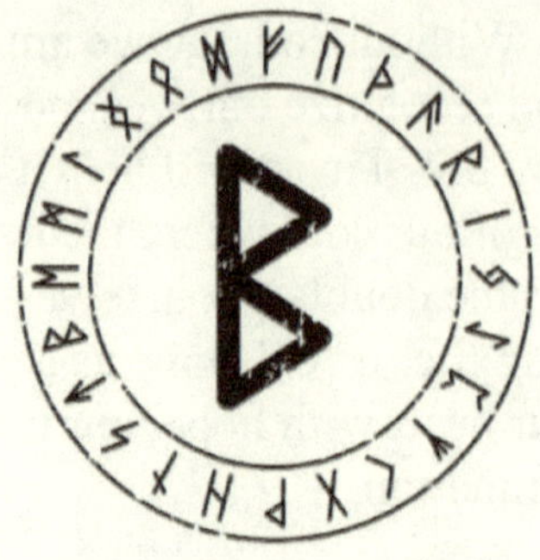

Berkano

Rebirth, healing, safety, growth, fertility, renewal

"The destiny of a child lies in the womb of its mother."

Berkano is the eternal vessel of creation, the sacred pulse of life itself. It is the force that births all existence, tenderly cradling the fragile spark of becoming within the infinite womb of divine love.

Berkano speaks to the soul's sacred journey - a continual unfolding through cycles of death and rebirth, where the essence of who we are is nurtured into being. Berkano reveals that true healing is not a return to what was but a transformation into what is destined to be. In its embrace, we are sheltered, not from challenge, but from despair, as it reminds us that every trial is the soil from which new life emerges.

It is the divine feminine, the presence that holds us in grace as we grow. Its protection is not a barrier but an invitation to step into the fertile unknown, where the seeds of our highest selves are planted. In Berkano, we find the sacred rhythm of existence - a profound trust that within the stillness of the womb lies the vast expanse of creation itself.

Berkano whispers that all beginnings are holy, and all endings are but portals to renewal. It is the essence of life's infinite becoming, the promise that what is nurtured in love will always find its way to the LIGHT!

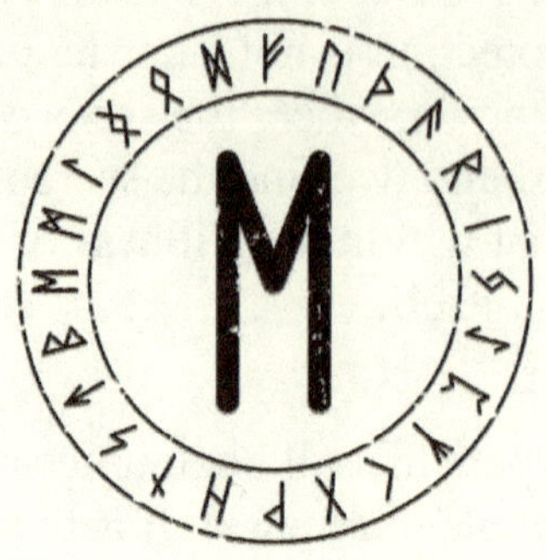

Ehwaz

Trust, loyalty, partnership

"The mind will trust the body, body will trust the mind."

Ehwaz is the rune of trust and loyalty. Perhaps these two qualities are the most desired and sought after in a relationship. When we forge a bond with another, we step out of the world we have built for ourselves and into the shared space of another's creation. In this merging of worlds, something far greater is born - a union of souls that transcends individuality and builds a new reality founded on trust and loyalty.

Trust allows us to expand without resistance, dissolving barriers and opening pathways to growth and unity. Through this expansion, we become more than we were, as trust and loyalty create fertile ground for deep connection. Whether between a man and a woman, a human and an animal, or any kindred spirits, partnership is built on the mutual exchange of these virtues.

In partnership, we discover strength and fulfillment, a sacred reflection of the divine unity that underlies all existence. Division is but an illusion, and unity is our true nature. Ehwaz reminds us that trust and loyalty are not just the building blocks of relationships but the very essence of our journey toward oneness with the source.

Ehwaz invites us to honor the bonds we share, to nurture trust and loyalty as sacred, and to embrace the divine harmony found in true PARTNERSHIP!

Mannaz

Mind, memory, learning, self-realization

"We are each a savior, each a god. It is the fear of what this means which binds us to the realm of humankind."

Mannaz is the rune of self-realization. It represents the essence of consciousness manifested in physical existence - flesh and blood brought to life by divine awareness. It symbolizes the bridge between the intangible and the tangible, the infinite and the finite, reminding us that our mind governs our physical reality.

Realizing consciousness in physical form becomes the spearhead for expressing our divine essence. Through this realization, we unlock the potential for inner growth and self-expansion. Mannaz calls us to see ourselves as creators of our experiences, capable of shaping our destiny through awareness and intentional action.

In this physical form, we are gifted with the unique abilities of observation and expression. Observation serves as the foundation of knowledge; it requires us to be fully present, to perceive without judgment, and to absorb the world around us. From this state of heightened awareness, we are empowered to choose our expressions wisely, aligning them with our authentic self. Through this harmony between observation and expression, wisdom emerges - a gift born of mindfulness and intentionality.

Mannaz nurtures a balanced and healthy state of mind, encouraging clarity and focus. It promotes the cycle of learning through observation, realization through awareness, and expression through action. This sacred process helps us embody and articulate our true selves, bridging the gap between potential and realization.

Mannaz guides us to walk the delicate path between ignorance and wisdom. It serves as a reminder that self-realization is not just a destination but an ongoing journey - a dance of discovery, understanding, and transformation. Through Mannaz, we learn to navigate through existence with grace, finding balance and **WISDOM** in the process!

Laguz

Water, subconscious, imagination, dreams

"Our future selves call us from infinite past, and each night are eroded with our dreams."

Laguz is the rune of all potentials in life. Our subconscious mind is like the vast ocean. All life originates from the ocean, just as all of our ideas and dreams originate from the subconscious mind. Without water, there is no life; without the subconscious mind, there is no reality. The deep, vast oceans of this world are teeming with a wide variety of life - most of it still undiscovered. Likewise, our subconscious mind is filled with ideas and potentials not yet realized in this world.

Laguz helps us immerse ourselves in the depths of our subconscious mind and reveal the potentials hidden beneath the field of our vision. We can extract these ideas and bring them to the surface, revealing them to the world. It takes time for them to materialize, so patience is essential.

Just as the surface of the ocean evaporates under the heat of the sun, our potentials are born into this world in a high vibrational state that is, at first, invisible. As the vapor forms into clouds, our ideas begin to take shape. The clouds grow denser until rain begins to fall upon the mountains - our ideas and potentials taking form and influencing the world. The rain gathers into a creek that gains momentum and flows down the mountainside. The tiny creek, faced with pebbles, rocks, and boulders, moves around them and relentlessly finds its way forward - just as our momentum carries us past obstacles.

Over time, the creek becomes a vast river, moving pebbles and rocks, pushing boulders, and carving entire canyons. As our potentials become fully realized, they have the power to change the world.

Water is life, life is movement, movement is PROGRESS!

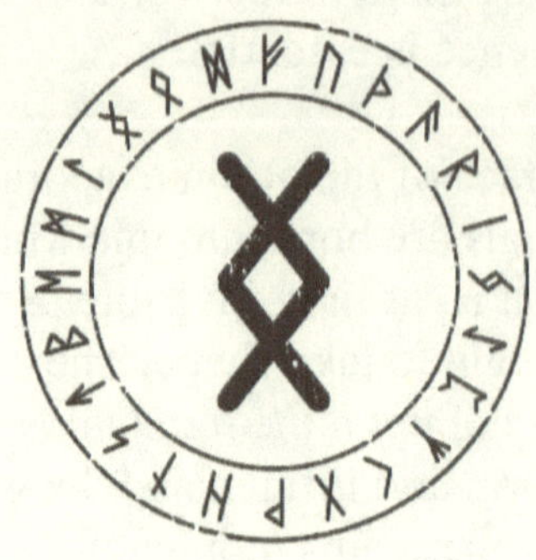

Ingwaz

Seed, gestation, creation, process

"Only when we know our solitude to be different from loneliness can we be whole enough to honor another's place."

Ingwaz is the rune of gestation. When a seed is placed into the earth, it seems to disappear, yet beneath the surface it begins its sacred work. It absorbs the warmth, moisture, and nourishment from the soil, slowly preparing for the moment it will break through into the light. This process cannot be rushed. Every second that passes, every shift beneath the soil, is part of the unseen miracle of becoming.

Ingwaz reminds us that growth is not always visible, but it is always happening. Just like the seed, we too are constantly changing, evolving, and preparing for the next stage of our unfolding. We often look to the past or the future, forgetting that all transformation happens in this very moment. The magic of creation, the magic of becoming, is happening *now*! In this everlasting moment of *now*, we develop and move closer to the realization of our true potential.

Through Ingwaz we begin to understand that we are part of a divine process of creation that never ceases. For our time here on Mother Earth, we are growing and developing within her living womb. Every experience, challenge, and joy nourishes us as we mature into what we are meant to be.

Ingwaz teaches us to trust the timing of our own becoming, to honor the stillness between what was and what is yet to come, and to remember that the power of life is always unfolding in the forever **NOW**!

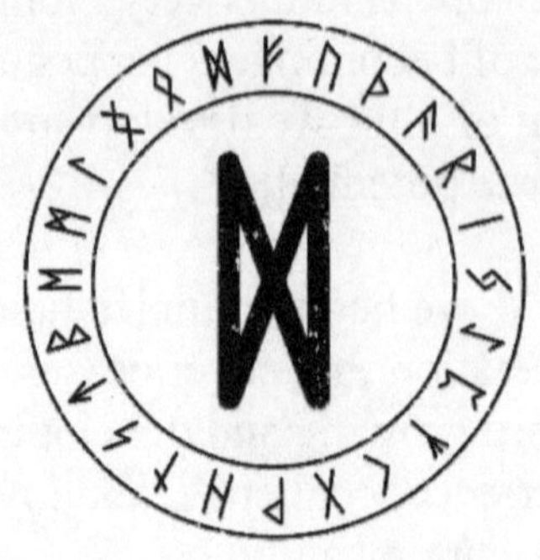

Dagaz

Day, awakening, enlightment

"Time is an illusion that once realized, is lovingly embraced, none the less."

Dagaz is the rune of the awakening consciousness. It represents the twilight between night and day - the sacred moment when darkness gives birth to light. It is the space between what was and what will be, the still point of creation, the everlasting *now*. Dagaz is balance itself—the meeting place of right and wrong, shadow and light, ignorance and wisdom. It is the spark of awareness that bridges the unknown and the known. It is the greatest gift we are ever given. It is *today.*

Today is the only day that truly matters. The past is gone, the future is uncertain, but today stands before us, alive and full of endless potential. We may carry lessons from yesterday and dreams for tomorrow, but all power lies in this single breath, this single heartbeat, this single moment. Today we can live, love, create, dream, and act. Today we can *be.*

Dagaz is the rune of transformation through balance. It is the light of understanding that dawns after the long night of confusion. It is where duality merges into clarity - where the mind and heart unite, where imagination and reason dance together to form the vision of what can be. In this merging, we awaken to truth.

Dagaz is the hourglass turned sideways when time stops and in this moment we are fully, completely **AWAKE**!

Othala

Inheritance, legacy, ancestry, home, family

"We inherit ourselves."

Othala is the rune of inheritance and ancestry. We are here today because our parents gave us life. They passed on to us the best they knew and the best they could. They, too, received the same from their parents, and this sacred exchange continues, flowing endlessly through the mists of time. Othala reminds us that we are the living continuation of all who came before us - their hopes, struggles, and triumphs live within us.

As we express ourselves in this world, we co-create reality through our thoughts, actions, and interactions with one another. The deepest and most meaningful of these interactions happen within the family. Family is where we experience our greatest love and often our greatest challenges. These strong emotions shape us, anchor our experiences deep within our being, and echo through generations to come.

The successes and failures of our ancestors still resonate in the great hall of our divine soul, where all memories of our lifetimes are gathered. Within this sacred space lies the vast and beautiful storehouse of the human experience - a place where our lineage and spirit intertwine. Through Othala, we gain access to this well of wisdom and memory, awakening the ancestral knowledge that flows through our blood and spirit.

Othala is the sacred enclosure, the spiritual home of the soul. It is the rune of belonging, heritage, and roots. It connects us to the lifeline of our family - the thread that ties the seeds of our soul to this world.

To understand Othala is to understand that we are never alone; we carry within us the breath, the strength, and the spirit of countless GENERATIONS who lived, loved, and dreamed before us.

III.

How do the runes work?

The runes serve as more than just symbols; they act as bridges connecting our conscious intentions with the vast, powerful knowledge of the subconscious mind. To understand how this works, it's important to see that our reality - everything we experience and see - is shaped by what's happening within us. This idea, championed by Neville Goddard in the 1920s and echoed by scientific findings in quantum theory in the 1950s, suggests that physical reality is, at its core, a field of limitless possibilities that come into form through our awareness and focus.

The subconscious mind, which is deeply connected to everything in existence, operates beyond the limits of time and space, and it doesn't view reality as "outside" of itself. It understands the nature of all things, including the runes. Each rune is like a doorway to this deeper understanding, a kind of symbolic language the subconscious can interpret and act upon. Since the subconscious is always aware and connected to all things, it recognizes the runes as holding certain energies or meanings.

When we use the runes, we're engaging our subconscious mind, sending it our intentions in a form it can understand. Each rune has a unique meaning - such as protection, growth, or transformation - and by focusing on a specific rune, we align our intentions with its energy. This allows our subconscious to pick up on and act upon these intentions, influencing the world around us.

Working with the runes is like opening a channel between our conscious desires and the subconscious mind's vast wisdom. When we focus on a rune, we invite its power to affect our life, bringing insight, guidance, or even change in our circumstances. This practice turns runes into tools that help us shape our own reality by allowing our conscious intentions to resonate within the subconscious, which continuously influences and shapes our experiences.

Just as ancient mystics viewed the runes as sacred whispers from the unseen, we too can see them as reflections of universal principles - energy patterns that correspond to states of consciousness. Each rune vibrates at a certain frequency, much like a musical note, resonating with particular emotions, archetypes, and forces of creation. When we meditate on a rune, draw it, or carry it with intention, we are essentially tuning ourselves to that frequency. The subconscious recognizes this resonance and begins to adjust our inner world to match it, drawing experiences, thoughts, and synchronicities that align with that vibration.

In this sense, the runes are not external powers that act upon us but mirrors of the inner creative process. They remind us that creation begins from within and that the universe responds to the patterns of belief, emotion, and focus we hold. When we cast or meditate upon runes, we are not predicting the future in a passive way - we are engaging in an active dialogue with the fabric of reality itself.

The more we work with them, the more the runes reveal layers of meaning that extend beyond words. They teach us to see the hidden order behind apparent chaos, to trust intuition as the voice of the subconscious, and to co-create with the forces that shape existence. In this way, the runes become not just tools of divination, but instruments of transformation - guiding us toward alignment with the deeper intelligence of life that speaks through symbol, rhythm, and **SILENCE.**

Meditation Insights

At the heart of my exploration of the runes lies a process that extends beyond the ordinary realm of thought and language. Much of what I've shared with you in these pages came to me through meditative states - states where the veil between worlds thins, and the messages of the runes reveal themselves not in words, but in pure understanding.

In these moments, as I entered a meditative state, I allowed my mind to slow, bridging the gap between the conscious and subconscious. With Viking ambient music playing softly in the background, and the calming scent of Palo Santo filling the air, I opened myself to the visions that came. In this half-alpha, half-beta brainwave state, pictures and symbols flowed quickly, beyond the confines of words. But it was through these images that the runes spoke to me.

As I emerged from the meditation, still connected to that space between worlds, I began to write. At that moment, what I had seen and felt began to take shape, becoming solidified in the act of recording it. The essence of the runes became clear. In writing, I was not just capturing thoughts; I was bridging the gap between what was seen in meditation and what could be expressed in this world.

This process was more than just intellectual - it was spiritual, almost like a form of channeling. And just as the runes revealed themselves to me, I believe that you, too, can access this ancient wisdom through meditation. After the exploration of the runes, I encourage you to embark on your own meditative journey, using the practices that resonate most deeply with you.

The following is an example of writing down our visions perceived through meditation about a specific rune for the day. The following vision took place on the morning of February 23rd, 2022.

The rune for the day was Ehwaz.

Ehwaz

Trust, teamwork, partnership

In my meditation, I saw a young child, about ten years old, on a field with tall grass. He was looking at me then he looked over my shoulder to my side on the right. He looked like he saw something extraordinary. His eyes were wide open from amusement. I followed his gaze to my right and saw a very tall old man standing next to me. He wore a light grey robe and a big hat. He had a long staff in his right hand and fashioned a long grey beard. I had the impression that he was Odin. He pointed over the distance, and beyond the endless field of grass, I saw a tall, rocky mountain covered with a snowcap. It looked challenging and gloomy, with dark grey clouds over it. The wind picked up, playing with the grass around me, and I felt a little threatened and uncomfortable by the thought of going there. A moment later, Odin pointed with his staff to the right of the mountain, where I saw the beautiful setting Sun over the sandy beach. It felt warm and looked very pleasant. I felt like he wanted me to choose which direction I want to go. I liked the thought of the challenging mountain but also understood that there is a much more pleasant way to go as well. I was tempted to choose the sunset but felt guilty for not accepting the challenge. I sat down to think about my decision for a while. Odin turned to me smiling and said: "You see, sometimes you need to allow yourself to accept and receive goodness, pleasantness, and abundance without the resistance of feeling guilty. There is absolutely nothing wrong with choosing the easy way!" I heeded his advice, and with an open heart, I headed in the direction of the beautiful sunset with Odin by my side.

True magic happens when we actually sit down and write down what we saw. When we do this right after our meditation, we still find ourselves in our alpha state of mind, in our receiving mode. Forming our visions into words is crucial, for it is the way to extract the revelations received through our meditation and manifest them into our physical world. As we write down our experiences, additional thoughts and ideas might follow that can help us understand better certain aspects of our life.

Contemplating the knowledge gained through meditation can immensely benefit our view of life and further our cause in this world.

In the final section of this book, I will share practical advice on how you can create the right environment for such meditative experiences: the music that calms and inspires, the scents that ground you, and the atmosphere that allows for deep introspection. These are the tools that worked for me, and I invite you to adapt them to your own spiritual practice. The runes have much to share, and through meditation, you can unlock their wisdom in a way that is personal and deeply **transformative**.

IV.

Step-by-Step Meditation for Connecting with the Runes

1. **Choose Your Rune**

The first step is to select a specific rune to meditate on. I highly recommend purchasing your own set of rune stones, either from a store or online. Once you've chosen your rune, hold the carved rune stone in your hand throughout the meditation. This physical connection helps deepen your focus and alignment with the rune's energy.

2. **Cleanse the Energy**

Begin by cleansing yourself and the space with Palo Santo. Light the Palo Santo and gently wave it around your body, allowing the smoke to purify your energy. Then, move around the room, cleansing the space where you will meditate. Envision the Palo Santo creating a protective bubble around you, clearing away any stagnant energy and preparing the atmosphere for deep connection.

3. **Enhance the Atmosphere with Incense**

After cleansing, light your incense cones. Choose masculine scents such as Copal or Dragon's blood - earthy and powerful smells that resonate with the Viking and Nordic energies. Let the incense fill the room, grounding you in the atmosphere associated with the runes.

4. **Choose Your Music**
Select Nordic ambient music to accompany your meditation. The music should evoke a sense of ancient wisdom and grounding, setting the mood and helping you enter a calm, focused state. Let it play softly in the background, enhancing the overall vibe and excitement of the practice.

5. **Find Your Center and Visualize**
Sit in a comfortable position, either cross-legged or with your feet flat on the ground. Close your eyes and take deep breaths, focusing on the rhythm of your breathing and the music. As you do this, press the tip of your tongue gently against the top of your mouth, just behind your upper teeth, and gently focus your eyes upwards toward your third eye.

You can interlace your fingers to create a circle and hold the rune stone between them, or you can rest your hands in a meditative position, touching your index fingers to your thumbs while holding the rune in one hand.

Begin visualizing a bright, goldish-whitish light above your head. This light represents the pure essence of the rune you are connecting with. See this light slowly spiraling downward, moving toward the top of your head. As it flows down over your shoulders, chest, and belly, feel it embracing and consuming you, filling you with calm, peaceful energy. Let it continue flowing down to your feet until your entire body is enveloped in this sacred light.

6. **Enter the Meditative State**
As the light consumes you, feel yourself becoming calm and relaxed, entering a deep alpha state. Now, visualize a staircase in front of you, leading down into the depths of your mind. Begin counting backward from 10 to 1, imagining yourself walking down the stairs. With each

step, feel yourself going deeper into your consciousness. When you reach the count of 1, you will be in your inner temple, your place of deep knowledge and connection.

7. **Open Yourself to the Rune's Essence**

By the time you reach the bottom of the staircase, you will be in a deep meditative state where you can start communicating with the essence of the rune you've chosen. Stay open to any symbols, messages, or feelings that come to you during this time. Trust the process, and let the rune reveal its wisdom.

8. **Record Your Experience**

Once the meditation feels complete, slowly bring yourself back to full awareness while maintaining the connection to the meditative state. Begin writing down the visions and thoughts that came to you, trusting the flow of your words. The act of writing will solidify the messages of the runes, bridging the gap between the meditation and your conscious understanding.

9. **Reflect on the Meaning**

After writing down your experience, take time to reflect. What do these visions mean to you? How does the meditation resonate now that it's been recorded? This is where the true message of the runes will begin to unfold.

Deepening the Connection: Entering the Rune Field

Every rune holds an ancient vibration - a pulse that predates language and thought. When you meditate upon a rune, you are not merely imagining it; you are stepping into a stream of consciousness that has flowed through centuries. The more often you enter this space, the more the runes begin to recognize you, responding to your presence with growing clarity.

After completing the steps of your meditation, remain seated in stillness for a few minutes longer than feels necessary. Do not rush to open your eyes or move. Let the silence expand until it feels almost alive. You may begin to notice subtle sensations - warmth in your hands, tingling at your forehead, or a sense of gentle pressure around your heart. These are the energetic signatures of the rune aligning with your own field. Simply observe them without expectation.

At this stage, you are not trying to "do" anything. You are listening with your entire being. This is the realm where understanding no longer comes through words but through resonance.

The Inner Vision Process

When the rune's energy begins to move, it may take form through symbols, colors, sounds, or even faint whispers. Every person receives differently. Some may see a vivid image; others may simply sense an emotion or feel drawn toward a certain direction of thought.

If nothing appears, do not worry. The runes do not always speak in obvious ways. Their messages often surface later - through dreams, synchronicities, or conversations that mirror the energy you invoked. Trust that your consciousness has been touched, even if your mind cannot yet translate the message.

If you wish to amplify your receptivity, try the following technique:

1. **Breathe through the Rune.** Visualize inhaling through the rune symbol itself - drawing its essence into your heart - and exhaling through your crown, releasing light into the world.
2. **Name the Rune Silently.** Whisper its ancient name inwardly. Let its sound vibrate in your chest like a chant. Each rune name is a frequency key that awakens memory within the soul.
3. **Ask the Rune Directly.** Formulate a simple question: "What do you wish to teach me?" Then release all effort. Allow whatever arises to unfold naturally.

Remain here as long as you feel held in its presence. The moment you sense completion - a deep exhale, a release of warmth, or a quiet knowing - thank the rune silently and begin to return.

Returning to Waking Awareness

When your meditation feels complete, take three long, grounding breaths. Feel the weight of your body and the surface beneath you. Wiggle your fingers and toes. Imagine any excess energy gently flowing down into the earth, where it will be transmuted into strength and balance.

If you feel slightly disoriented, drink water or touch a piece of wood or stone to anchor yourself. The contrast between the inner and outer world is natural; you have just crossed between realms. Over time, this transition becomes smoother, like waking from a vivid dream while keeping its wisdom intact.

Writing as Ritual

When you begin to write about your meditation, do so without analysis. Let your pen move freely. Capture the raw impressions first - images, sensations, words, and emotions. Only afterward begin to reflect on their meaning.

This writing process is not a report; it is a continuation of the meditation. You are translating vibration into form. You may find that as you write, new insights appear - sometimes entirely different from what you experienced during meditation. This happens because the act of writing activates another level of consciousness: the bridge between vision and manifestation.

To preserve the energy of your experience, consider keeping a dedicated **Rune Meditation Journal**. Start each entry with the date, the rune's name, and any preliminary feelings before meditation. Then document what you saw, heard, or sensed. Close with reflections, lessons, or affirmations. Over time, this journal becomes your personal grimoire - an unfolding dialogue between your soul and the ancient runic current.

Integrating Rune Energy into Daily Life

Meditation is not meant to end when you open your eyes. The true purpose of this practice is to embody the rune's wisdom throughout your day. Each rune corresponds to an archetype, a lesson, and a state of being.
For example:

- **Fehu** teaches flow and stewardship of energy - practice generosity and gratitude.
- **Ansuz** opens communication - listen deeply and speak truthfully.
- **Raidho** governs movement - take one purposeful action aligned with your intuition.
- **Berkano** nurtures growth - attend to something that needs gentle care.

After your meditation, choose one small action that expresses the essence of your rune. This is how spiritual practice becomes living wisdom. Through consistent embodiment, the runes evolve from symbols on stone to forces alive in your daily existence.

The Gate of the Heart

While many focus on the mind's imagery during meditation, the deepest connection occurs in the heart. The heart is not only the emotional center but an organ of perception - capable of sensing truth before the intellect does. When the rune energy flows through your heart, you may feel warmth, expansion, or tenderness.

Allow this feeling to deepen. Visualize the rune symbol within your chest glowing softly with each heartbeat. This visualization activates coherence between your heart and mind, allowing understanding to rise effortlessly. The runes then cease to be external wisdom - they become part of your inner voice.

The Voice of the Ancestors

The runes are a bridge between your consciousness and the ancestral field. Every time you meditate upon them, you attune to the memories of those who walked this path long before you. You may sense presences - guides, teachers, or ancestors - standing quietly nearby.

If you do, greet them with respect. They appear not to command but to remind you of forgotten knowledge encoded in your DNA. In these moments, insight often comes as intuition rather than speech: a knowing that feels ancient and familiar.

Remember to thank them silently at the end of your practice. Gratitude strengthens the link between worlds and invites continued guidance.

Working with the Breath of the Rune

In Norse tradition, breath is sacred - the breath of life, *ond*, given by the gods. To connect more deeply with a rune, pair your meditation with intentional breathing:

1. **Inhale:** Imagine drawing in the rune's light.
2. **Hold:** Let its energy settle in your chest.
3. **Exhale:** Send the rune's wisdom outward, blessing your surroundings.

Repeat this cycle nine times, symbolizing the nine realms of Norse cosmology. With each breath, the rune becomes more alive within you, forming an energetic pattern that continues to vibrate long after the session ends.

Entering the Visionary State

With continued practice, you may begin to experience the *liminal space* - a state between waking and dreaming where consciousness expands. The boundaries of the physical world soften, and imagination merges with revelation. In this state, you may perceive scenes, symbols, or beings like the child and Odin in the Ehwaz vision.

These are not random fantasies. They are the language of the deeper mind communicating through metaphor. Every vision holds meaning tailored specifically for you. Ask inwardly, "What truth are you showing me?" and feel the answer rather than forcing logic upon it.

Over time, you'll learn to recognize the quality of true rune communication: it carries peace, wisdom, and empowerment - never fear or confusion.

Closing the Sacred Space

When your meditation and journaling are complete, it is important to close the energy properly. Extinguish the incense consciously. Whisper gratitude to the elements that assisted you - Fire for transformation, Air for clarity, Water for intuition, and Earth for grounding.

You may place your rune stone back into its pouch or on your altar, symbolizing the completion of the exchange. As you do, affirm silently:

"The wisdom received today anchors within me.
I walk in balance, guided by the ancient light."

This seals the practice and ensures that the energy remains harmonized rather than scattered.

The Cumulative Power of Practice

Like any spiritual discipline, consistency is key. The first few meditations may feel quiet, but with each session, your sensitivity grows. Over time, you will begin to notice that the rune energies appear spontaneously - in dreams, coincidences, or sudden insights during ordinary moments. This is a sign that your consciousness has merged with the runic field.

Each meditation builds upon the last. Think of them as stepping stones across a river; every step brings you closer to the far shore of self-knowledge and mastery.

Reflection

Through meditation, you are not merely studying the runes - you are remembering them. You are awakening an ancient dialogue between the finite and the infinite, between human awareness and divine pattern.

Every rune you connect with reveals a mirror of your own being. What you see within it is, ultimately, yourself - the eternal consciousness exploring its own mystery through symbol and experience.

When approached with reverence, patience, and openness, this practice becomes more than meditation. It becomes communion.

Common Sensations During Meditation

When connecting with the runes, different practitioners experience a wide range of sensations. Understanding these helps distinguish authentic energetic shifts from simple relaxation responses.

- **Vibrational Tingling:** Often felt in the hands, forehead, or chest. This is the rune's frequency resonating through your subtle body.
- **Temperature Fluctuations:** Sudden warmth or coolness indicates energy flow. Warmth often accompanies activation; coolness signals release.
- **Visual Flashes or Colors:** The subconscious translates rune energy into light patterns. For example, Sowilo may appear as golden light, while Isa may present as silver or pale blue.
- **Auditory Echoes:** Humming, distant tones, or rhythmic pulses correspond to runic harmonics within your nervous system.
- **Emotional Waves:** The runes clear old imprints. Tears, laughter, or sudden calm are signs of alignment, not imbalance.

When these sensations occur, do not resist or chase them. Simply observe, breathe, and let them pass through you. Awareness itself integrates the energy.

Symbol Interpretation Guide

During meditation, the subconscious speaks through archetypal language. The same image can carry different meanings for different people. The key is *relationship*, not fixed symbolism. Still, the following guide can assist beginners:

- **Mountains** – challenge, growth, higher vision
- **Rivers** – flow, adaptability, emotional release
- **Fire or Light** – purification, awakening, divine spark
- **Animals** – instinctive power or guardian aspects
- **Doors or Gates** – transition between phases
- **Ancient Figures** – ancestral wisdom, inner teachers

When a symbol appears, ask silently, "What aspect of me does this represent?" The answer will arise as a feeling or thought. Note it, but avoid rigid conclusions. Meaning matures over repeated meditations.

Rune Meditation Journal Prompts

After each session, record your impressions using prompts that draw wisdom into conscious clarity:

1. What was my physical and emotional state before beginning?
2. What sensations or images emerged most vividly?
3. What message, feeling, or theme stood out?
4. How does this connect to my current life situation?
5. What small action or mindset shift can honor this message?
6. What synchronicities or changes appeared afterward?

You may revisit earlier entries after several weeks. Patterns will reveal themselves - certain runes appearing during similar life phases, recurring symbols marking transformation, or even subtle cycles of growth aligning with lunar or seasonal rhythms.

Creating a Personal Rune Altar

To strengthen the continuity of your practice, dedicate a small space to your rune meditations. This altar acts as a physical anchor for the energies you invoke. Include:

- A **cloth** or board marked with the rune symbols most meaningful to you.
- **Natural elements:** a stone (Earth), candle (Fire), bowl of water (Water), and feather or incense (Air).
- Your **rune set** or a single rune stone of focus.
- A **journal** and **pen** reserved solely for this work.

Each time you meditate, light the candle, breathe consciously, and acknowledge the sacredness of this connection. Over time, this space will accumulate a tangible stillness - a threshold between worlds.

Extending the Practice Beyond Meditation

Once you feel comfortable entering rune consciousness, you can incorporate it into motion and creativity:

- **Runic Walking:** As you stroll outdoors, mentally chant the name of your chosen rune with each step. Feel its rhythm merge with your heartbeat.
- **Runic Drawing:** Sketch the rune slowly, focusing on intention rather than artistic perfection. The act of forming it by hand strengthens neural and energetic associations.
- **Runic Breathwork:** With each inhale, imagine the rune's shape forming inside your lungs; with each exhale, project it into the world as radiant light.
- **Runic Affirmations:** Transform the rune's essence into personal declarations such as "I act with right will" (Tiwaz) or "I allow change to refine me" (Dagaz).

These extensions integrate the runes into everyday awareness, ensuring their wisdom remains active beyond the meditation mat.

Seasonal and Lunar Cycles

Ancient practitioners often aligned their rune work with natural rhythms. You can enhance your connection by timing meditations with specific cycles:

- **New Moon:** ideal for invoking new beginnings - Fehu, Uruz, or Berkano.

- **Full Moon:** suited for illumination and revelation - Sowilo, Ansuz, or Dagaz.
- **Solstices and Equinoxes:** times of balance and transformation - Jera, Raidho, or Othala.

Mark these dates in your journal and note how each season influences the tone of your meditations. Nature mirrors the same runic cycles within your psyche.

Final Reflection

Each meditation opens another doorway between you and the ancient current of wisdom woven through creation. When practiced consistently, you begin to sense that the runes are not static symbols carved into stone but living energies echoing within every cell of your being.

The true aim of this practice is integration - to live as the embodiment of runic awareness.
To think with clarity like **Ansuz**, act with courage like **Tiwaz**, love with depth like **Gebo**, and transform with grace like **Dagaz**.

In doing so, meditation ceases to be an occasional ritual and becomes a way of seeing the world: every sound, movement, and encounter a rune in motion - each one whispering the eternal language of creation.

V.

The Art of Casting the Runes

The Sacred Act of Casting

There comes a moment, just before a rune touches your hand, when the world around you seems to quiet itself. The air grows still, as though creation holds its breath, waiting for you to reach into the unseen. This moment - the moment before the cast - is where the true magic begins.

Casting runestones is not a mechanical act or an intellectual exercise. It is an intimate meeting between your deepest self and the ancient forces that dwell beneath the roots of Yggdrasil. Unlike rune cards, which speak in images the mind can quickly grasp, the stones speak in weight, in presence, in the silent language of earth and time. They are shaped not merely by hands, but by the spirit of the one who seeks.

When your fingers enter the rune bag, something subtle happens. Your thoughts - normally sharp and restless - begin to soften. The chatter fades, the surface stills, and from within the quiet emerges another voice… older, wiser, familiar. It is the voice of your own subconscious, the hidden well of intuition that has always guided you, even when you did not know how to listen.

The act is simple. Yet its meaning is infinite.

The runes themselves do not command power. They carry it - gently, faithfully - like messengers who know exactly where they must go and what they must reveal. Their power comes from the alignment between your intention and the great field of possibility that envelops all things. The stones open the door; your awareness steps through it.

In truth, casting the runes is a conversation between three forms of yourself: the seeker who asks, the listener who receives, and the ancient one within who already knows.

To cast the runes is to return to that ancient one - to remember what wisdom feels like before it becomes words.

Preparing the Self

Before you allow the runes to speak, you must first become the kind of listener they trust.

There is no need for robes, incense, or ceremony unless they stir something sacred within you. What the runes truly require is sincerity - a willingness to approach them not as tools, but as teachers.

Sit quietly. Let your body settle into the earth beneath you. Allow your breath to find its natural rhythm, as though you are remembering something you once knew but long forgot.

Feel the weight of the moment.
Feel the questions that have followed you through the day.
Feel the truth within you that has waited -patiently -for the chance to rise.

Before casting, ask yourself softly:

Am I prepared to hear what I do not expect?
Am I willing to receive the truth rather than the answer I desire?
Am I ready to face myself with honesty and humility?

For the runes do not bend to comfort.
They do not flatter, nor do they soften their message to spare your pride.
They reveal what *must* be understood -not to wound you, but to free you.

Enter the casting not as a desperate seeker, but as a traveler approaching a sacred well. Bring openness. Bring stillness. Bring respect.

And when your breath settles, when the world around you grows quiet, the runes will reveal themselves not as stones, but as mirrors.

Preparing the Runestones

Your runes are more than carved symbols. In time, they become companions on the path - silent allies who learn the shape of your spirit.

Before you cast them, hold the rune bag gently in both hands. Feel its texture, its quiet weight. Allow the warmth of your palms to seep through the fabric. This moment of contact is a kind of greeting, an unspoken acknowledgment that something sacred is about to begin.

Touch the stones one by one.
Let them warm in your hands.
Let their edges bring you into presence.

Runes absorb energy - your energy.
They remember your hopes, your fears, your questions, your hesitations. Just as the World Tree remembers the footsteps of the gods, the stones remember the hands that hold them. The more you work with them, the more attuned they become to the rhythm of your inner world.

A scattered mind produces scattered answers. A clear mind, clear messages.

Treat your runes with respect and they will respond in kind. They are not lifeless artifacts. They are doorways - small, silent, powerful.

Over time, you will feel them awaken, each stone carrying a subtle pulse of recognition, as though they have begun to understand the language of your soul.

The Metaphysics of Rune Casting

Behind every casting lies a meeting of forces - your intention, your awareness, and the vast field of possibility that surrounds all life. This field is not metaphorical. It is the very fabric of reality, a vibrating sea of potential described by ancient mystics and now glimpsed by modern quantum science. Every thought, every emotion, every subtle movement of consciousness exists as a ripple within this field.

Intention is not a wish. It is not the flicker of a fleeting thought.
Intention is the steady flame in the center of your being - the quiet truth you hold beneath all other truths, the coherent signal that rises above the noise of the thinking mind.

In metaphysical traditions, intention is understood as a force of alignment: the act of tuning yourself to a particular frequency of reality. In quantum physics, a parallel concept emerges in the observer effect -the strange truth that the act of observing shapes the outcome. Before observation, any particle exists in a state of pure potential, a cloud of possibilities. Only when observed does it take on a definite form.

When you cast the runes, your intention acts as this observer.
Not by force, but by resonance.

Your intention spreads outward like ripples across a still lake, creating a subtle disturbance in the field around you. It reaches into the depths of your subconscious, into that vast inner cosmos where memory, intuition, and archetypal wisdom intermingle. Here, beneath the surface of ordinary awareness, the runes begin to respond -not to what you think, but to what you vibrate.

This is why the conscious mind does not choose the rune. The intellect is too narrow, too linear, too bound by expectation. The rune is chosen by the part of you that sees without eyes - the deeper intelligence that interacts with the quantum field long before the mind can interpret it.

In this invisible meeting between intention and possibility, the rune emerges as the physical expression of an inner truth. It collapses the infinite spectrum of potential meanings into a single symbol, a focal point through which insight can flow. The act of reaching into the rune bag becomes a moment of quantum selection, where the unseen harmonizes with the seen, and the symbol that rises is the one that carries the exact frequency of your question.

This process -so effortless, so natural -echoes the mysteries at the heart of reality. The moment you seek clarity, life responds. The moment you touch the unknown, the unknown arranges itself into something knowable. The moment your awareness enters the field, a new thread of understanding begins to weave itself into form.

You do not choose the rune. The rune chooses itself through you.

This is the quiet miracle of casting: a communion between the outer hand and the inner truth, between matter and consciousness, between the visible and the unseen.

It is a moment where time folds in on itself - where the past that shaped your question, the present that carries it, and the future implied within it gather into a single point of awareness.

This is why rune casting feels both ancient and immediate, mystical yet grounded. It speaks to the part of you that remembers the language of symbols, that understands reality not as a fixed structure but as a fluid interplay between what is known and what is possible.

Rune casting teaches a profound truth: that wisdom is not something you chase, but something you allow.

The runes reveal not what the world imposes, but what your soul already knows - waiting for the moment when intention, awareness, and the great field of possibility briefly align.

Rune Casting Through the Lens of Norse Cosmology

To understand the deeper nature of rune casting, one must look not only into the quantum field or the subconscious mind, but also into the ancient cosmology from which the runes emerged. The Norse did not view the world as a single, linear dimension but as a living tapestry woven across nine interconnected realms - all suspended within the great branches and roots of Yggdrasil, the World Tree.

In Norse cosmology, every event, every symbol, every thought exists not in isolation but as a thread in the vast, breathing fabric of existence. The runes themselves are not mere marks carved into stone; they are *primordial forces*, fragments of the ordering principles that shape the cosmos. They arose from the very moment Odin glimpsed the hidden patterns beneath creation, patterns that still pulse through the branches of the World Tree.

When you cast a rune, you are engaging with these patterns.

You are touching not just a symbol, but a vibration—a resonance that echoes through all nine realms:
Midgard, where humans walk;
Asgard, home of the gods;
Vanaheim, realm of the Vanir;
Alfheim, realm of the light elves;
Svartalfheim, home of the dwarves;
Jotunheim, land of the giants;
Helheim, realm of the dead;
Niflheim, the world of frost;
Muspelheim, the world of fire.

These realms are not distant places.
They are dimensions of experience, woven into the psyche, each expressing a different facet of existence.

Your subconscious mind moves through these realms effortlessly.
Your emotions echo through them. Your intentions ripple across them.

This worldview is strikingly similar to what quantum physics now proposes: that reality is not a simple, physical landscape but a multi-layered continuum, a set of overlapping fields where energy becomes matter, thought becomes form, and possibility narrows into the event we perceive.

When a rune is cast, it is as if a signal is sent through the branches of Yggdrasil - a request for insight, a question that travels along the invisible pathways that bind the worlds together. And in response, the appropriate rune emerges, not by chance, but through resonance.

The symbol that rises is the one aligned with your current position in the cosmic web.

This is why the runes feel alive.
Why they speak with such clarity.
Why they reveal not only answers, but connection.

In Norse cosmology, fate is not a rigid chain of predetermined events. Fate - *Urðr* - is woven in real time by the Norns beneath the roots of Yggdrasil. They draw from past, present, and future simultaneously, because these states are not separate. They intertwine like the strands of a single thread.

This is the same truth quantum physics hints at when it dissolves the boundary between past and future, suggesting that time is not a line but a unified field.

Thus, when a rune falls before you, it does not simply reflect a future possibility.
It reflects the entire pattern - your past choices, your current energy, and the destiny you are leaning toward.
It shows what the Norns might be weaving in this moment.

Rune casting becomes an act of perceiving the tapestry before the pattern fully forms.

It is a glimpse into the living architecture of fate, filtered through the symbol that best matches your inner vibration. A rune appears because it resonates with your energy across the nine realms, across your subconscious, across the quantum field where all possibilities exist.

This is why the runes speak with such authority - not because they command the future,
but because they reveal the structure of the moment from which the future will grow.

Each cast is a meeting place:
where ancient cosmology and modern science overlap,
where the branches of the World Tree and the waves of the quantum field mirror one another,
where intention shapes reality,
and where the runes answer not with prophecy, but with truth.

In this light, rune casting becomes more than divination.
It becomes a form of cosmic alignment - a moment in which the seeker, the symbol, and the great woven universe become one.

Basic Casting Styles

The ancient traditions offer many ways to receive the runes. Each method opens a different doorway into the self.

1. The Single Rune Draw

The simplest casting, yet often the most profound.
A single rune is like a solitary torch carried into the darkness—one symbol, one message, one truth.

This draw is ideal for daily guidance or moments when life feels tangled and you long for clarity. By removing complexity, the single rune reveals the essence of your situation, cutting through confusion like a blade through fog.

It does not shout.
It whispers.

And in that whisper, you will find exactly what you need.

2. The Three-Rune Cast

Here, the runes unfold like a story.

The first rune shows the root- what brought you here.
The second reveals the energy shaping your present.
The third shows how the current is flowing, and where it may lead if unaltered.

But the beauty of this cast lies in its flexibility.
You may also use it for:

You - Challenge - Way Forward
Body - Mind - Spirit
Shadow - Lesson - Integration

This cast paints a picture - not only of events, but of the heart and soul beneath them. It is a gentle guide for moments of transition, confusion, or deep reflection.

3. The Five-Rune Cross

This is the compass of the runic world.

Center: the heart of your situation
North: what uplifts or guides you
South: what challenges or burdens you
East: what is rising on the horizon
West: what is fading or must be released

The Five-Rune Cross gives you a panoramic view of your inner and outer worlds. It shows movement - what pulls you forward, what holds you back, and what stands at the threshold of becoming.

It is the map you consult when the road ahead branches in many directions.

4. The Nine-Rune Spiral

Nine - the sacred number of Odin's sacrifice and the deep cycles of life.

Casting nine runes into a spiral shape opens one of the oldest forms of divination. Only the face-up runes speak, and their placement reveals layers of meaning.

Closest to you lie the truths of your inner world.
Midway sit the energies currently shaping your path.
Farther away lie the whispers of the future, forming quietly in the mists.

Runes that overlap share a common thread - fate entwined with fate.
Runes far apart speak of influences distant yet powerful.

Reading the nine-rune spiral feels like listening to the pulse of the world.

5. The All-Cast (Full Rune Throw)

There are moments when you seek not guidance but revelation - when the whole tapestry of your life pulls at your spirit.

In such times, cast all twenty-four runes.

Let them fall as they wish, forming clusters, lines, isolations, and patterns that speak with the raw honesty of the divine. One rune may fall off the cloth entirely—an intruder from the edges of fate. Another may land atop its sibling, doubling its message.

This casting is not delicate. It is thunder. It is truth in its ildest form.

Use it when you are ready to see the full constellation of your destiny.

Freestyle Casting (Intuitive Casting)

This is the casting of the mystic.

No spreads. No structure. No rules.

Hold your question not in your mind, but in your heart. Let it settle. Let it become a quiet flame within you. Then reach into the bag and draw runes as intuition guides you.

Draw until something in your spirit says, *Enough.*

This form reveals what the intellect cannot grasp:
your fears, desires, blind spots, potentials, forgotten truths.

Freestyle casting does not speak to the mind.
It speaks to the soul.

The Freehand Method

One that bridges inner sensing with outer ritual.

Glide your hand slowly above the runes or over the bag. Move with patience, with presence, with trust. You are not searching; you are listening with your skin.

A subtle shift will come: a warmth, a tingle, a gentle pull, a sudden stillness.

In that moment of quiet alignment, choose the rune beneath your hand.

This method teaches true intuition - the kind that does not rise from thought,
but from the deep and ancient place where the runes themselves were born.

Advanced Casting Techniques

Casting for Decisions

When life divides into paths, the runes illuminate the soul of each choice. They show not only where a path leads, but who you become by walking it.

This is the wisdom the mind often forgets.

Casting for Emotional Healing

Runes reveal the roots of wounds - old stories, old fears, old echoes carried through years.

By casting for the emotional root, the release, and the rebirth, you walk the inner path toward wholeness.

Casting for Shadow Work

The shadow is not darkness.
It is unrecognized light.

This casting reveals what you have not yet allowed yourself to see, and how to bring that lost part of you home again.

Casting for Manifestation

Manifestation is the marriage of belief and readiness.

The runes reveal what you believe, what you fear, and what you are prepared to receive.

Casting for Cycles and Timing

Some doors open only when the soul is ripe.

The runes reveal when an energy is ending, beginning, or not yet ready to emerge.

Why Rune Casting Works: A Deeper Explanation

Rune casting operates on many layers, weaving science, psychology, myth, and spirit into one cohesive truth.

Psychologically, the runes bypass the conscious mind.
Emotionally, they reveal truths the heart carries.
Energetically, they respond to your intention.
Quantum theory tells us observation shapes outcome.
Archetypally, the runes awaken ancient memory.

The runes do not show a fixed future.
They show the river beneath your feet the current, the pull, the direction.

Change the current, and the future changes with it.

Bringing It All Together

The runes are not fortune-tellers. They are lanterns guiding you deeper into yourself.

To cast them is to enter a sacred dialogue a moment where your inner world speaks in the timeless language of symbols.

The runes reveal the architecture of your spirit:
your truths, your shadows, your patterns, your power.

Once you learn to listen, the runes will show you that wisdom was never beyond reach.

It lived within you all along waiting for the moment you were ready to hear it.

VI.
Casting the Runes for Others

"There are moments in life when two paths meet for a reason—
when one heart seeks clarity
and another becomes the quiet channel through which truth may speak."

Casting the runes for someone is not simply a reading.

It is a conversation between two subconscious minds, guided by symbols older than memory and carried on the currents of breath, intention, and presence.

To read for another is to step into a sacred exchange. It requires clarity, grounding, and a willingness to listen not only with the ears but with the entire inner being.

This chapter is a guide a steady, simple, and authentic way to invite wisdom into the space between two souls.

Casting the runes for another person is one of the most intimate forms of intuitive work. It requires preparation, focus, openness, and a respectful understanding of how human energy and the subconscious mind interact. What follows is a complete guide to how I personally cast the runes - step by step - so that anyone reading this book can learn to do it with integrity, clarity, and depth.

Choosing and Preparing the Rune Stones

The process begins with selecting your set of runes. Choose stones that resonate with you, green for peace, aquamarine for clarity, or any material that feels aligned. The color or stone type is a personal preference, but each material carries its own subtle energetic signature.

Once chosen, the runes must be cleansed.

All objects absorb energy. They collect impressions from the environments and hands they pass through. Before using the runes for intuitive work, they should be returned to a neutral energetic state.

I prefer Palo Santo for this. I light it, let the smoke rise, and gently pass each stone through it.

From a metaphysical and scientific perspective, scent and smoke shift the brain's wave patterns. Aromatic compounds interact with the limbic system, altering the emotional state and aligning the subconscious mind with the task at hand. Cleansing the runes clears stagnant energy and prepares both the stones and the mind for a clear channel of information.

This resets the runes, making them fully receptive to the intention of the reading.

Preparing Yourself Before the Reading

Before casting for someone else, I set my own internal state.

I wear clothing that aligns me with meditation or spiritual focus. Clothing is symbolic: it signals to the subconscious mind that we are stepping into a different mental space. This change in appearance shifts the internal identity into the role of the rune reader.

Interestingly, the day before a reading, I often begin feeling the presence of the person I will be casting for. Images, impressions, or thoughts about their life rise naturally.

This happens because intention creates an energetic link.

When we focus on someone, the subconscious extends into the unified field, the interconnected web of consciousness. Thinking about a person pulls their presence into our awareness. This is why people often call or message us at the moment we think of them. Consciousness is relational.

Setting the intention to perform a reading opens the channel long before the guest arrives.

Creating the Atmosphere

On the day of the rune casting, the space becomes the foundation of the entire experience.

Every environment holds energetic residue from conversations, emotions, and events. To ensure clear and undistorted information, the space must be reset.

I cleanse the room again with Palo Santo or sage. Then I set the atmosphere:

Music
Ancient Nordic ambient tones or meditative music. These vibrations anchor the mind, slow the breath, and create coherence between you and your guest.

Scent
I burn dragon's blood or copal, deep, grounding, earthy scents. Female practitioners may choose softer scents. The only rule is resonance.

Casting Cloth
I place a rune cloth on the floor between myself and the guest. This becomes the symbolic field where the subconscious reveals patterns through the stones.

Before my guest arrives, I sit in silence for a moment, letting my mind release everyday concerns.
A calm mind becomes a clear channel.

Guiding the Guest Into the Subconscious

When the guest arrives, I seat them across from me.

The clearest readings happen when both the reader and the guest enter a shared meditative alignment. This allows intuition to rise and the subconscious mind to speak more freely.

I guide the guest through a simple relaxation:
Close the eyes

Relax the body

Visualize a glowing white or golden light above the head

Watch the light slowly descend, calming the body part by part

Once the light reaches the feet, I guide them down a staircase, counting from ten to one. At the bottom is a door.
When they open it, they symbolically enter their subconscious mind.

I follow the same visualization myself.
This synchronizes our inner states.

When both of us are in this deeper awareness, the casting can begin.

The Heart-Centered Question

Once we reach the subconscious doorway, I give the guest a quiet moment.

Then I ask:

"What is the most concerning trouble that weighs on your heart?"

Not the mind, the heart.

Often their answer changes from what they expected before the session.
This is the true question, the genuine concern.
This is the doorway the runes will speak through.

Drawing the Runes

As they express their concern, I begin swirling my hand through the runes.

I do not think. I do not search. I simply let the hand choose.

Whatever I grab is what was meant to be grabbed.

In a meditative state, the body becomes an extension of the subconscious mind. Artists, athletes, and performers often achieve impossible feats by letting the subconscious guide the body. Rune casting works the same way.
The subconscious guides the hand to the runes that carry the message.

I cast them onto the cloth between us. This begins the reading.

Interpreting the Spread

This is where knowledge and intuition intertwine.

As the ancient poem warns:

"Let no man carve runes to cast a spell,
Save first he learn to read them well."

Once the runes are cast, the pattern reveals the story.

General guidelines:

Runes farther from you often represent past influences, hidden roots, or the deeper cause of the concern.

Runes closer to you reveal the immediate energy, the outcome, or the action required.

Clusters indicate intertwined forces or repeating cycles.

A rune alone at the edge signals an unseen influence or an external factor.

But beyond structure, the true reading comes from intuition.

In a meditative state, the runes do not speak as separate symbols. They speak as patterns. As living archetypes.
As the unfolding story of the person sitting before you.

The messages come as impressions, knowing, and clarity that blend your subconscious alignment with the symbolic language of the runes.

Closing the Reading

Once the message is expressed clearly and calmly, without exaggeration or fear, the stones are gathered respectfully. The active channel of communication has finished its work.

The guest leaves with clarity, guidance, and a sense of direction. The reader, however, must ensure one final step.

Detaching Your Energy After the Reading

This is essential. During the casting, you and your guest share a subconscious connection. Your intuitive field absorbs pieces of their emotional atmosphere. If not released, these fragments can weigh you down and cloud your own life.

To detach safely and professionally:

Step One: ***Return to the Body***

Place your feet firmly on the ground. Feel your weight. Awareness of the body commands the subconscious to return to your personal field.

Step Two: ***Reverse the Light***

Visualize the same light you used during meditation rising back up through your body.

As it rises, it pulls back any energy that does not belong to you.

Step Three: ***Cut the Energetic Thread***

See a thin, soft thread of light between you and the guest.

Gently "cut" it with your hand, with your breath, or simply with intention.

This signals the subconscious mind to close the channel.

Step Four: ***Ground With Breath***

Exhale slowly and release any residue.

Breath resets the nervous system and restores emotional equilibrium.

Step Five: ***Seal the Space***

Cleanse the runes briefly.

Then say softly or mentally:

"Thank you. The session is closed."

This seals the energetic field and restores neutrality.

Why Detachment Matters

When two people enter a shared intuitive state, their fields overlap. Thoughts, emotions, and subconscious impressions flow freely.

Detachment ensures that:

Your clarity remains intact

Your emotional field stays clean

You do not carry another person's burden

Your intuition stays sharp for future readings

It preserves the integrity of both the reader and the guest. Casting the runes for another person is an act of service.

It is a moment where intuition, openness, and compassion meet.

The runes speak through us, but they do not belong to us.

We become the bridge steady, clear, grounded between a seeker and the wisdom they are ready to receive.

When the session ends, we return to ourselves, intact and centered, leaving the guest with clarity and carrying only gratitude forward.

VII.

Final Words: Walking the Path of Wisdom

The runes are not just tools of divination; they are living expressions of consciousness. Each time you hold a rune, you are holding a fragment of the universe's language a note in the grand symphony of creation.

Approach them with reverence but also with curiosity. The runes are teachers, not judges. They meet you where you are, revealing only what you are ready to understand.

When used with patience, sincerity, and a heart open to transformation, the runes become more than symbols they become companions on your journey of awakening.

May this book serve as your guide as you learn to read the silent language of creation

the whispers of the runes.

About the Author

Tibor Tamas Farkas is a Hungarian-American entrepreneur and writer drawn to the mysteries of consciousness and the unseen patterns that shape our lives. Since his youth, he has explored the relationship between thought, intuition, and reality, seeking to understand how inner awareness gives form to the world around us. Guided by curiosity and a willingness to take bold steps, Tibor approaches life as both an adventure and a lesson in trust following the quiet call of the heart wherever it leads. Whispers of the Runes is a reflection of that journey, blending insight, courage, and wonder into a single thread of discovery.

www.ingramcontent.com/pod-product-compliance
Lightning Source LLC
LaVergne TN
LVHW090528110826
845146LV00003B/1023

* 9 7 9 8 9 9 5 0 6 3 3 1 5 *